DIWALI

Kerena Marchant

CARNIVAL

CHINESE NEW YEAR

CHRISTMAS

DIWALI

EASTER

HARVEST

ID-UL-FITR

PASSOVER

Editors: Polly Goodman/Sarah Doughty
Designer: Tim Mayer

First published in 1996 by Wayland Publishers Ltd
61 Western Road, Hove, East Sussex BN3 1JD

This edition published in 1999 by Wayland
Publishers Ltd

Find Wayland on the Internet at
http://www.wayland.co.uk

British Library Cataloguing in Publication Data
Marchant, Kerena
  Diwali. – (Festivals)
  1. Diwali – Juvenile literature
  I. Title
  394.2'682'94536

ISBN 0 7502 2532 7

Printed and bound by Eurografica S.p.A., Italy

Author's acknowledgement: Thanks to my
Hindu friends who have shared their festival
celebrations and culture with me – Amarjit Ram,
Champa Swift and the Modi family.

Picture acknowledgements
Cephas/M. Dutton 29 (bottom right); Circa Photo
Library 13 (bottom),19 (top), 24 (top), 25,/Bipin J
Mistry *cover* (top left),/John Smith *cover* (top
right); Hutchison Library/Liba Taylor 15 (top),
/McIntyre 29 (bottom left); James Davis
Worldwide Photographic Library 5, 11; Eye
Ubiquitous/David Cumming 10,/Tim Hawkins 23,
/Pam Smith *cover* (centre); Life File/Andrew Ward
12, 23 (top), *cover* (bottom right); Bipin J Mistry
18 (bottom), 27; Christine Osborne 7, 18 (top), 20
(top), 22 and *title page*; Ann and Bury Peerless 16,
20 (bottom); Trip/Dinodia 6, 13 (top) and *cover*
(bottom left), /H Rogers 8, 9, 13 (top), 14, 15
(both), 17 (bottom), 26, 29 (top),/L Clarke 21
(top). Border artwork is by Tim Mayer.

CONTENTS

DIWALI AROUND THE WORLD

Since the Second World War, many Indians have come to Britain. In the 1950s a shortage of labour brought Indians to Western countries. In 1972 the ruler of Uganda, Idi Amin, forced the Indian workers to leave and 25,000 fled to Britain. Today, Britain has the largest population of Hindus outside India.

BRITAIN

In about AD 500 Hindu traders crossed the Himalayas to bring Hinduism to Assam and Sikkim and the island of Ceylon (Sri Lanka). By AD 900 traders had brought Hinduism to the Himalayan kingdom of Nepal.

Traders crossed the Indian Ocean in around AD 900 to bring Hinduism to Thailand, Malaysia, Cambodia and parts of Indonesia. Today the main religion of Indonesia is Islam, and only a small area east of Java is Hindu, including Bali.

In recent years, Indians have migrated to the Gulf states where they can earn more money than in India.

GULF STATES

INDUS VALLEY

NEPAL

Indian labourers built railways in East Africa. In the nineteenth century Indians emigrated to Kenya and Uganda. They were invited by the British to build roads.

UGANDA

KENYA

THAILAND

SRI LANKA

CAMBODIA

MALAYSIA

Hinduism began around 2000 BC in a part of India called the Indus Valley. Today this includes part of Pakistan and the Indian province of Punjab. Over the next 2,000 years, Hinduism spread all over India.

JAVA **BALI**

Indians were recruited to work in Natal in South Africa and the island of Mauritius in the nineteenth century, mainly to work on plantations.

MAURITIUS

NATAL

The majority of Hindus in the USA are Americans who join the community of monks at Diwali as part of the Krishna Consciousness movement in New York.

NEW YORK CITY

Indians went to the Caribbean (Trinidad) and Guyana in the nineteenth century because the owners of sugar plantations needed workers after slavery was abolished. The majority of Hindus in the Caribbean came from Bengal.

TRINIDAD

GUYANA

All around the world, fireworks are lit to celebrate Diwali.

Indians came to the South Pacific (especially the Fiji islands) in the nineteenth century to find work on sugar plantations. Indians make up 50 per cent of the population of Fiji today.

FIJI ISLANDS

Map showing the main areas of migrations and settlement from India.

WELCOME TO DIWALI

Diwali is a Hindu festival and the themes of Diwali tell us about what Hindus believe. Hinduism centres around the worship of God, who can be worshipped in different ways though different Hindu gods. The most important thing for a Hindu is to love and please God – by living a good life, by setting up shrines at home, by frequent prayers and by celebrating the many Hindu festivals. Diwali is such a festival.

Diwali is the Hindu festival of light. The word Diwali is short for dipawali, which means 'row of lights'. Diwali is celebrated during late October or early November, when it gets dark early and the nights are cold, long and dark. Hindus enjoy preparing for festivals as much as they enjoy celebrating them. They can start preparing for Diwali a month before the festivities begin and the celebrations can last for up to 5 days.

Traditional clay lamps, called diwas are placed at doors and windows throughout the festival of Diwali.

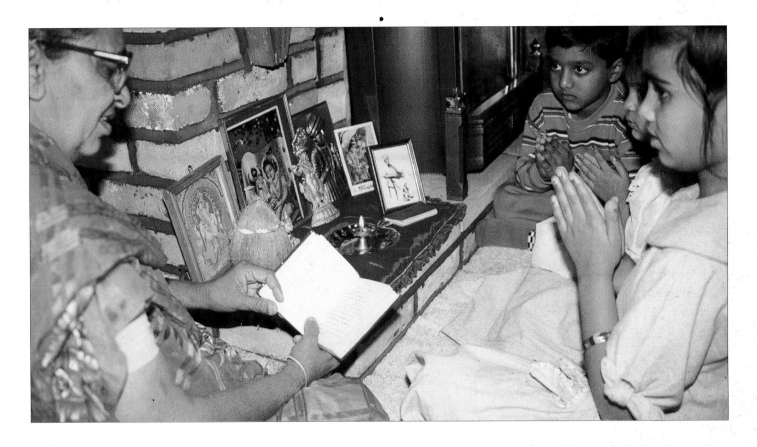

The Hindu gods are part of the family and have their shrine in the living room, where they can be included in family events and where it is easy to gather every day to pray. On the shrine there are pictures and statues of different gods including Krishna and Ganesh.

At Diwali, the dark nights are lit up. Houses have welcoming lamps at all their doors and windows, and multi-coloured lights decorate the streets. The temples are covered with tiny rows of lights and the sky is ablaze with fireworks. Shop windows are piled with different-coloured sweets and everybody wears their brightest clothes.

Diwali is celebrated for different reasons all over India because different gods are honoured in different areas. However, all the different Diwali festivities have a lot in common. They celebrate the triumph of good over evil, light over darkness, life over death. It is a time of hope and new beginnings.

DIWALI GODS

The main characters of the Ramayana: Rama, Lakshmana and Sita. Hanuman kneels at their feet. It is easy to see which one is Rama because he is usually painted blue to show that he is an incarnation of Vishnu.

On each day of Diwali, different gods are remembered and each area of India has its own favourite gods. One of the most popular Hindu gods is Vishnu and most Hindus remember Vishnu's good works at Diwali.

Legends about Vishnu tell how he cared for the world and would come down to earth to defeat evil. Vishnu would be born on earth as a human being or an animal, in a process called incarnation. Hindus call Vishnu's incarnations avatars, which means 'descent'.

Incarnation involves a god experiencing the love, pain and suffering of the life of that human being or animal. Vishnu had many incarnations on earth, as a fish, a boar, a tortoise and a dwarf. He also became human many times, such as when he became Prince Rama and Krishna.

A favourite Diwali story about Vishnu is taken from the Ramayana, an ancient Hindu poem. It tells how Vishnu became incarnated and lived on earth as Prince Rama. Prince Rama was the eldest son of a king in north India. Rama's wicked stepmother wanted her son to become king instead of Rama, so she exiled Rama from the kingdom for 14 years. During his exile Rama lived in a forest with his wife, Sita, and brother, Lakshmana.

One day, a demon, called Ravana, kidnapped Sita and took her to his island. Rama and Lakshmana raised an army and went to rescue Sita. In a battle, Rama killed Ravana with a magic bow and arrow and rescued Sita. By then Rama's exile was over and he could become king. To welcome Rama back to his kingdom, people lit lamps along the roads and at every window.

The most important thing a Hindu can do is to show love and devotion to the gods, like the woman above. The god Krishna is playing his flute. Like Rama, he is painted blue to show that he is an incarnation of Vishnu.

It was a time of new beginnings because the evil demon was slain and there was a new king.

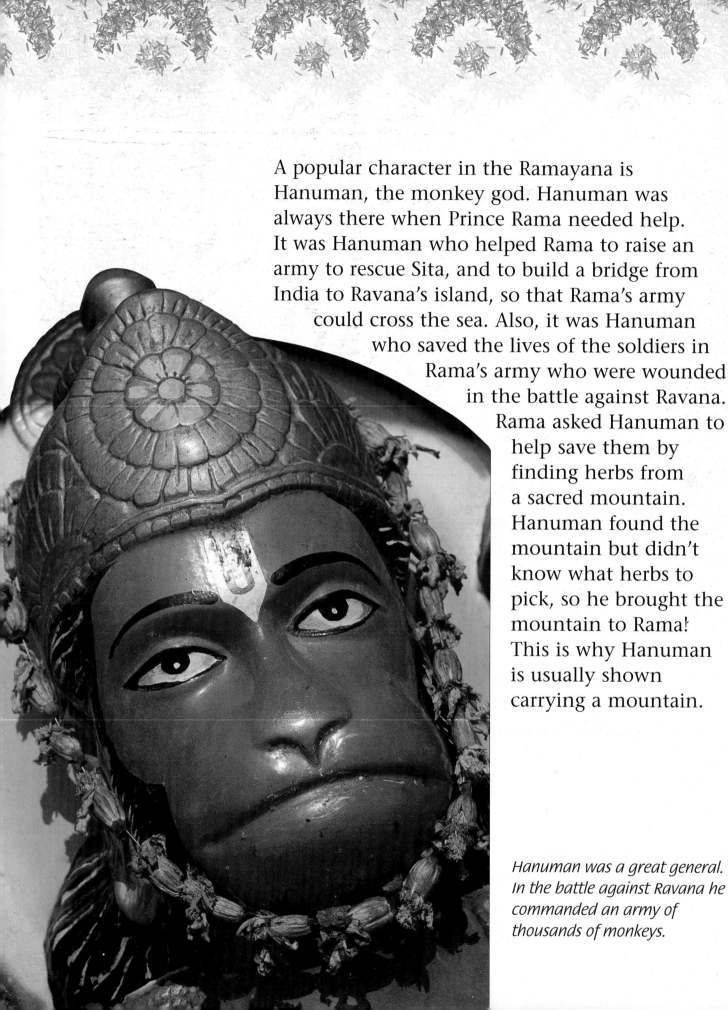

A popular character in the Ramayana is Hanuman, the monkey god. Hanuman was always there when Prince Rama needed help. It was Hanuman who helped Rama to raise an army to rescue Sita, and to build a bridge from India to Ravana's island, so that Rama's army could cross the sea. Also, it was Hanuman who saved the lives of the soldiers in Rama's army who were wounded in the battle against Ravana. Rama asked Hanuman to help save them by finding herbs from a sacred mountain. Hanuman found the mountain but didn't know what herbs to pick, so he brought the mountain to Rama! This is why Hanuman is usually shown carrying a mountain.

Hanuman was a great general. In the battle against Ravana he commanded an army of thousands of monkeys.

Many people light fireworks at Diwali to celebrate the burning of Ravana's kingdom by Hanuman. Ravana captured Hanuman and set his tail on fire. Hanuman escaped by leaping out of the window and jumping across the houses, setting everywhere on fire.

Hindus honour Hanuman's courage and loyalty to Rama by not killing monkeys. Thousands of monkeys live around Hindu temples and are fed by the worshippers and priests.

During Diwali, families light sparklers in their back gardens and courtyards. There are also large fireworks displays in temples, where rockets and Roman candles are used.

CANDLES AND LIGHTS

The weeks leading up to Diwali are a busy time for the potters in India, who have to make thousands of clay lamps called diwas. On the first day of Diwali everybody buys a new lamp to represent new beginnings.

In some rural parts of India there is no electricity. Few roads have street lights, so thousands of lamps are a welcome sight to travellers on the dark roads. The lamps at the doors of the houses help visitors to find the house they are visiting and this is the real significance of the lamps. They are there to welcome visitors and, at Diwali, Hindus expect some very special visitors.

The temples outshine all the other buildings in towns and villages at Diwali. They are often decorated with rows of tiny electric lights and give a magical feel to the festivities.

AN UNWELCOME VISITOR

There is one person that the lights do not welcome – the demon, King Bali. Before Vishnu killed King Bali, Bali pleaded with Vishnu to allow him to continue to rule on earth, but only for one day a year. Vishnu agreed and allowed him to rule for one day at Diwali, but only in places where no lamps were lit.

The lights in this busy Bombay temple are both decorative and functional. They light up the stalls selling garlands of flowers to the worshippers.

On the first day of Diwali only one lamp is lit. This is to welcome Yama, the god of death. Diwali is the only time when Yama is honoured and the spirits of the dead can return to earth. The single lamp is said to help the souls of dead to find their former earthly home. On the following days of Diwali all the lamps are lit. People hope that the god they are remembering will see the lights and pay them a visit.

Diwali has been affected by modern times. Multi-coloured electric lights are now used to decorate streets in towns all over India. In countries such as Britain and Canada, it is easy to spot Hindu areas in towns (for example Leicester and Vancouver) by the Diwali street lights. Temples are also covered in tiny rows of electric lights and many families put fairy lights round their windows. People still buy lamps for traditional reasons, or use metal diwas.

Many families put metal lamps like these on their family shrines.

WEALTH AND PROSPERITY

The day that the Diwali lights shine at their brightest is on the goddess Lakshmi's birthday. Lakshmi is the wife of Vishnu.

According to legend, Lakshmi was born in the ocean. When she was born lots of treasures came out of the ocean, so she is the goddess of wealth and good fortune. Hindus believe that a Diwali visit from Lakshmi will bring them luck and wealth in the year to come.

Hindus do everything they can to persuade Lakshmi to enter their house. They leave all the doors and windows open and make sure there are shining lights at every door and window, so that Lakshmi can easily find them.

The goddess Lakshmi is usually drawn holding a conch shell and a lotus flower, which are her symbols. In this picture she is flanked by the 10 incarnations of her husband, Vishnu.

Nobody tries harder to lure Lakshmi to their houses than the villagers in Andhra Pradesh, in south-east India. They build bamboo platforms outside their houses and at night, the women sit on the platforms holding flaming torches and singing hymns to Lakshmi.

Diwali cards showing the goddess Lakshmi, a pot of money and the god Krishna.

Everybody wants to impress Lakshmi when she visits, so the household account books are put out for her to inspect. And all bills are paid! Gifts of money or jewellery are left out on an altar for her.

In Gujerat, in west India, Diwali is the start of the new business year. All businesses close their account books and present them to Lakshmi. Everybody wants to do well at work and Diwali is the time to make that happen. Hindus always visit the people they work with at Diwali and during these visits, Sukh Diwali (Happy Diwali) cards and presents are exchanged.

In Nepal students raise money at Diwali. They gather at street corners singing songs while they beg for money to fund their studies or to give to charity.

The ceremony of the closing of the accounting year. The businessmen have red marks on their foreheads to show that they have completed the prayers that form a part of the ceremony.

GOOD LUCK ?

Gambling is a popular Diwali pastime. The town or village squares are crowded with groups of people playing cards. Everybody believes that Lakshmi will bring them luck. But there are always losers, even at Diwali!

CLOTHES AND BODY DECORATIONS

The traditional Hindu dress for women is a sari. Unmarried women can wear a dress over loose trousers. Most women wear lots of jewellery – brightly coloured bangles, earrings and nose studs. On special occasions, like Diwali, they draw henna patterns on their hands and feet.

Hindu men are becoming more Westernised in their dress but festivals are occasions when men do wear more traditional clothes. In northern India, this is a loose tunic worn over trousers. In southern India, men wear dhotis, which are body wraps tied around the waist. In many areas men wear brightly coloured turbans.

Everybody buys new clothes at Diwali. In many areas of India there is a special day at Diwali when brothers give their sisters new saris and sisters give their brothers new shirts.

A woman from Rajasthan in northern India with henna patterns on her hands.

Much of the Diwali preparation concerns clothes. Villagers put aside time to journey into the big towns to buy material. Hindus living outside India ask friends or relations going on holiday to India to bring back some material for them. Sometimes they will get Indian fashion magazines sent to them and make new clothes themselves.

As much as 5 to 8 metres of material is needed to make a sari.

Indian people love colours. The people who dye material are always looking for new ideas and colours. Some dyers are so skilled they can dye material with different colours on each side. Printers also print patterns on the fabric using carved wooden blocks.

The amount of gold thread on a sari can give the sari its value. It is not uncommon to weigh a sari to determine how much it is worth!

Many people buy material and decorate it themselves. Each area of India does this differently. In Rajastan, it might be tie-dyed. In Benares, gold and silver thread is sewn on to the silk. In Bengal, cotton is decorated with tiny mirrors and sequins.

F O O D

Hindu cooks take great pride in their cooking and often dye the food they have prepared with bright colours to make it look more attractive. It is then placed in colourful plates and garlanded with flowers and tinsel.

Food plays an important part in all Hindu festivals and Diwali is no exception. Visitors are expected throughout the Diwali festival, so lots of food is prepared.

Hindus have strict rules about food, and many Hindus will only eat food that is prepared by their family or friends. Whenever Hindus went to live outside India, they would never eat the local food and always cooked the type of food they ate when they lived in India. As a result, Hindu food is similar throughout the world.

Hindus have a great respect for life and don't like killing animals, so most Hindus are vegetarian and don't eat meat.

Lots of different foods including curry, rice, naan bread and raitha are eaten together on a special plate called a thali.

The national meal of India is curry but this is not anything like the curry served at school meals. Curries are made from about 30 different spices and flavourings and every region has its own recipes. In southern India there are sambars in Karela; aviyals in Andhra Pradesh and vindaloos and madras curries in Tamil Nadu. In northern India there is rogan josh in Kashmir and korma and pasanda in Uttar Pradesh. All are made with plenty of chillis and most are hot to eat.

Curries are eaten with bread or rice. Popular types of bread are naan bread or chappatis. In northern India, pillau rice, flavoured with spices is popular. Southern Indians flavour their rice with coconut, lemon or mango.

Hindus love sweet desserts, such as rice puddings or cheese balls in a sweet syrup called rassogolla. Normally desserts are only eaten at festivals and special occasions. The rest of the time Hindus will end their meal with fresh fruit. No meal is complete without a drink of lassi, which is a yoghurt drink. Lassi can be flavoured with sugar or salt and is said to help the body digest food.

Eastern snacks meet Western snacks! Hindu children combine traditional pakoras with sandwiches, crisps and chocolate cakes.

Guests who aren't invited for a formal Diwali lunch or dinner are never sent away hungry. They are given snacks, or 'tiffin' as they are called in India. These are usually deep fried and made in advance. Popular tiffins are samosas, poppadums, bajias and pakoras. In southern India pancakes made from lentils, called dosais, are a popular snack.

The most important Diwali food is sweets and everybody exchanges gifts of sweets at Diwali. Hindus believe that gifts of sweets encourage people to think sweet things about them. Hindu sweets differ all over India. Some are like toffee or fudge; others are deep fried and covered with a sweet syrup.

DIWALI TRADITIONS

Hindus start every day of Diwali with a bath. After this members of the family massage scented oils into each other's hair. It is then time for prayers at the family shrine. Every Hindu home has a number of shrines to different gods all over the house.

Festive garlands on sale in a market outside a temple.

After the prayers the festivities begin and family and friends call round. Everyone may go out for the day. A favourite visit is to the local Diwali market, where there are stalls selling sweets, flowers and jewellery, camel and elephant rides and actors act out the Ramayana story. There is also village dancing for everyone to join in. As soon as it gets dark everybody goes home for an evening of feasting and fireworks.

As the dark night falls, Indonesian Hindu families in Bali and Java gather under a huge screen, lit by an oil lamp. Soon, shadowy finger puppets fill the screen, acting out stories from the Ramayana.

In India the focus of the Diwali festival is the home, not the temple. Diwali is a time for family gatherings and for entertaining friends.

Decorating the courtyard of a house in Tamil Nadu in South India with rangoli patterns. The women are making the pattern with white paste, which symbolizes purity.

A brightly painted shadow puppet, richly dressed for a festive occasion. The puppeteer moves the puppet behind a screen and the audience see only the puppet's shadow.

In the days leading up to Diwali, house-proud Hindus make sure that their house is ready to receive visitors. Every house is repainted and cleaned from top to bottom. There is also a religious reason behind the spring clean. One of the things that the god, Vishnu, did during his earthly incarnation as Krishna, was to kill Naraka, the demon of filth.

All over the Hindu world, people decorate the floors and pavements outside their houses with colourful rangoli patterns, and there are often competitions for the best patterns. Rangoli means 'mixture of colours'. The patterns are made from coloured rice-flour paste. Popular colours are red kum-kum and yellow turmeric, which are believed to drive away evil spirits. The patterns consist of sacred Hindu symbols such as the swastika, which stands for good fortune and god's blessing. Another favourite Diwali symbol is a lotus flower, the symbol of Lakshmi. People who draw a lotus flower hope that this will encourage Lakshmi to come into their house and sit on it.

RANGOLI PATTERNS

You can make your own rangoli patterns using coloured chalks. Always remember to ask permission before you draw these on pavements, driveways or in playgrounds. If you can't get permission, draw them on paper using coloured paint. Try and copy the following patterns.

 a swastika ... the symbol of good fortune and the god's blessing.

 om (pronounced ome)... a sacred Hindu word which means 'creation' or 'I Am'.

 the lotus flower ... the symbol of Lakshmi painted gold with a taper put in its mouth and set alight.

DIWALI IN THE TEMPLE

Outside India the temple is more important in the Diwali festivities than the home. This is because Diwali is not a long public holiday as it is in India and everybody has to go to work and school as normal. Hindus might live a long way from each other and will only meet up at festivals such as Diwali, so festivals are large community events. As the weather in Britain and North America is cold in winter it is best to hold Diwali events indoors and large temples are an obvious place to hold them.

In Hindu temples, statues of the gods are looked after by priests. They wake them in the morning, feed them during the day and put them to bed at night. At Diwali, the priests dress the statues in brightly coloured silk clothes, richly embroidered with gold and silver. Like everybody else at Diwali, the temple gods are expecting visitors.

Guests ring the temple bell to let the gods know that they have arrived, before they enter bringing gifts of sweets and garlands of flowers. There are no formal services, but every visitor says a private prayer to the gods asking for good fortune. In India, temple visitors would leave after this prayer to enjoy Diwali at home, but outside India, visitors will spend a day of festivities in the temple.

In Bombay, a temple visitor arrives in her best sari, with a plate of offerings for the temple deities.

Everybody brings plenty of food to the temple for the gods and for themselves. While everybody eats, musicians play traditional music and sing songs. The music is played on a sitar, an instrument that looks a little like a guitar, and a tabla, which is like a drum.

The altar in this temple is covered with offerings of sweets, fruit and cakes, carefully arranged by the priests.

Krishna Consciousness monks show their devotion to Krishna. They wear simple orange robes and shave their heads in the same way that traditional Hindu monks do.

KRISHNA CONSCIOUSNESS: DIWALI IN NEW YORK

In the USA the majority of Hindus are Americans who have become Hindus and belong to a Western form of Hinduism called Krishna Consciousness. At Diwali they join the community of monks and families who live full time in the Krishna Consciousness temple in New York. People wearing traditional Indian clothes and monks with shaved heads wearing orange robes sing songs to Krishna on the streets outside these temples.

The celebrations include feasting on traditional Hindu food specially prepared in the community kitchens, plays based on stories about Krishna and Prince Rama, and hours of devotional singing such as:

Hari Krishna, Hari Krishna
Krishna, Krishna, Hari, Hari

Hari Rama, Rama Rama
Rama Rama, Hari Hari.

After the meal, there is dancing. Older Hindus who remember life in India are always keen to teach the younger Hindus traditional dances, as they know this is the only way to keep traditions alive outside India. Festivals like Diwali are often the only opportunities that Hindus who have never lived in India have to learn the traditional dances. A popular dance in Diwali celebrations outside India is the dandia raas. Most Hindus are familiar with the dandia raas because there are regional variations of this all over India.

Children dressed as Krishna and Radha perform at Diwali.

In the dance everybody has a pair of sticks. They dance around a partner, tapping their partner's sticks to the time and rhythm of the music.

DIWALI IN TRINIDAD

In Trinidad, the island's Christian and Muslim communities join in the Diwali celebrations because they feel that themes of Diwali are important to them. Everybody puts up tall bamboo poles all over the island and clay diwas are attached to these poles. When Diwali comes, these diwas are lit. No effort is spared at Diwali as every building is covered with lights.

Hindu priests join with Muslim and Christian ministers to hold large Diwali services for everybody in public places. Candles and lanterns are lit as everybody celebrates the triumph of good over evil, and prays for wealth and good health.

After the services there is a carnival and Diwali queens and princesses are crowned. Hindu music plays long into the Caribbean night and the shimmer of the lights reflects across the waters, welcoming the Hindu gods to Trinidad.

As the music gets faster and faster, so does the banging of the sticks. Soon the room becomes a whirl of colour and the noise of the banging sticks drowns the music. The banging of the sticks reminds many people of how the Hindu gods drove evil out of the world at Diwali.

The climax of all these Diwali celebrations is a grand fireworks display. Roman candles and rockets light up the sky. But the celebrations don't end too late because everybody has to get up for work and school the next day.

Hindu children carefully copy their parents during the stick dance. If you make a false move, it is easy to hit someone or get hit with a stick.

SIKH DIWALI

The festival of Diwali is also celebrated by Sikhs. The Sikhs believe in one god and do not worship the Hindu gods. Their religious teachers are holy men called gurus. Sikhs celebrate Diwali because of events that took place during the life of the 6th Sikh Guru, Hargobind Sahib.

The Muslim emperor, Jahangir, who ruled in India from 1605-27, did not like the Sikhs or the Hindus. He decided to imprison the 6th Sikh Guru and 52 Hindu kings in his fortress. Many people begged the emperor to release the guru and eventually the emperor agreed. However, the guru refused to be released unless the Hindu kings were also freed. The emperor reluctantly agreed to this and the guru and the Hindu kings were all freed at Diwali.

The 6th Guru was both a saint and a soldier. He encouraged his followers to learn military skills such as swordsmanship to defend themselves against persecution.

The Sikhs were overjoyed when their leader was released and lit candles and lamps on the roofs of houses to guide him home to Amritsar in the Punjab. The Guru's mother was so pleased to see him, she ordered sweets and food to be given out to everybody. Sikh Diwali celebrations recall these events. Sikh Diwali is a three-day festival. The place for Sikhs to be during Diwali is the Golden Temple at Amritsar, which is lit with tiny rows of lights, and candles float in the lake. Sikhs who are unable to go to Amritsar at Diwali will have a model of the temple in their home, which is surrounded with candles.

The Golden Temple at Amritsar is the centre of Sikh worship. The 6th Guru built a fortress around it so that it could be easily defended.

At Diwali, Sikhs gather to worship at the Golden Temple, or a local Sikh temple, which is called a gurdwara. Everybody brings gifts of sweets, which are shared out. All the worshippers light a candle and sing hymns about how the 6th Guru fought for religious freedom, justice and equality for all. Every worshipper is always given free food in the community kitchens. The climax of the day at the temple is a grand fireworks display.

THE HINDU CALENDAR

There are many Hindu festivals. Different festivals take place all over India at different times. These are the main festivals that most Hindus will celebrate, but they will vary from region to region.

The Hindu calendar is different from the Christian calendar. There are 12 Hindu months. Each month has two halves of 15 days. The first half of a month is called 'the bright half' and the second half is called 'the dark half'. As the start and finish of each month is determined by the appearance and disappearance of the moon the dates of festivals vary from year to year.

Chiatra or New Year Festival
March to April
This new year festival marks the start of the Hindu calendar and is meant to bring good luck. Hindus celebrate by putting up a coloured bamboo pole with the following items tied to it – a brass pot, a garland of flowers, brightly coloured cloth and some sugar discs.

Rami Navami or Rama's birthday
April to May
A nativity festival a week after New Year's Day to celebrate the birth of the Rama. In temples a doll or coconut in a cot, with flowers, represents the baby Rama.

Ratha Yatra *June to July*
The Chariot or juggernaut festival worshipping Krishna; from the Hindu word Jagannath meaning 'Lord of the Universe'. Huge chariots with a statue of Krishna and decorations of flowers are pulled through towns in India.

Rakasha Bandhan or Sisters and Brothers day *July to August*
To drive away evil, sisters tie red and gold thread around their brothers' wrists. In return, brothers give presents to their sisters.

Janmashtami or Krishna's birthday *August to September*
Another nativity festival, to celebrate the birth of Krishna.

Ganesh-Chaturthi *August to September* ▲

A festival to honour the elephant-headed god, Ganesh, said to remove all obstacles.

Vavaratru/Dusserah/Durga Puja
September to October

A 9-day festival to worship the mother goddess and her victory over the buffalo demon. The goddess is also known as Durga Puja, Parvati, Kali. In other places it marks the victory of Rama over the demon king Ravana.

Mahashivratri *January to February*

A festival dedicated to the god, Shiva, particularly in north India. He is known as a creator god, as well as a god of destruction. There are aspects of good and evil in his nature. He is known as many things – the god of life, the god of death and the lord of the dance. Shiva is said to have created the world in a cosmic dance.

Holi *February to March*

One of the most popular festivals in India. A spring festival that celebrates the wheat harvest. A sacred bonfire is lit and everybody throws red powder and coloured water at each other. ▼

GLOSSARY

Amritsar
A city in the Punjab area of India that is important to Sikhs.

Bali
A demon king, who was killed by Vishnu. It is also the name of a Hindu island in Indonesia.

Gurdwara
A Sikh temple.

Guru
A Sikh holy man. There are 10 Sikh gurus. The book of Sikh scriptures is also a guru. It is called the Guru Granth Sahib.

Guru Hargobind Singh
The 6th Sikh Guru. His release from prison led to the Sikhs celebrating the Hindu festival of Diwali.

Incarnation
A process by which gods can live on earth as animals or humans.

Krishna One of the forms Vishnu took when he was incarnated on earth. Krishna is worshipped as the god of love.

Lakshmana
Rama's brother.

Lakshmi
The wife of Vishnu and the goddess of wealth and good fortune.

Naraka
The demon of filth, killed by Krishna.

Rama
One of the forms Vishnu took when he was incarnated on earth. Rama was a prince of a north Indian kingdom.

Rangoli Sacred patterns that are painted outside houses and in temples on special occasions.

Ravana The ten-headed demon, who kidnapped Sita, the wife of Rama, in the Ramayana.

Sanskrit An ancient language of India, used in the Hindu scriptures.

Sari
The traditional dress of Hindu women.

Sikhism
An Indian religion that began in the sixteenth century.

Sita
The wife of Rama, the heroine of the Ramayana.

Vishnu
A Hindu god who always saves the earth from evil.

Yama
The Hindu god of death.

BOOKS TO READ

A Flavour of India by Mike Hurst
(Wayland, 1998)

Celebrate Hindu Festivals by Dilip Kadodwala
and Paul Gateshill (Heinemann, 1995)

Celebration! by Barnabas and Anabel Kindersley
(Dorling Kindersley, 1997)

Feasts and Festivals by Jacqueline Dineen
(Dragons World, 1995)

Hindu by Anita Ganeri, *Beliefs and Cultures*
series, (Watts ,1995)

India by Susie Dawson, *Fiesta* series,
(Watts, 1998)

My Hindu Faith by Anita Ganeri (Evans,1999)

My Hindu Life by Dilip Kadodwala and Sharon
Chhapi (Wayland,1996)

My Sikh Life by Manju Aggrawal
(Wayland, 1996)

The World of Festivals by Philip Steele
(Macdonald Young Books, 1996)

What Do We Know About Hinduism? by Anita
Ganeri (Macdonald Young Books, 1995)

EXHIBITIONS OF HINDU ART

The British Museum, Great Russell Street,
London WC1. Tel: 0207 636 1555

The Victoria and Albert Museum, Cromwell
Road, London SW7. Tel: 0207 938 8500

MORE INFORMATION ON THE HINDU WORLD

The Commonwealth Institute, London W8
Tel: 0207 603 4535

The SHAP Working Party on world religions
can supply a calendar of religious festivals;
religious artefacts and photo packs on
different beliefs – The SHAP Working Party c/o
The National Society's RE Centre, 36 Causton
Street, London SW1P 4AU. Tel: 0207 932 1194,
fax: 0207 932 1199

Religious artefacts and posters can be bought
from Articles of Faith, Bury Business Centre,
Kay Street, Bury BL9 6BU. Tel: 0161 705 1878

Books and Hindu music can be bought from
the Institute of Indian Art and Culture, the
Bhavan Centre, 4a Castletown Road, West
Kensington, London W14 9HQ.
Tel: 0207 381 3086.

Krishna Consciousness, Correspondence
Secretary, Croome House, Sandown Road
Watford, Hertfordshire WD2 4XA

INDEX